Gases

William B. Rice

Consultant

Scot Oschman, Ph.D.
Palos Verdes Peninsula Unified School District
Rancho Palos Verdes, California

Publishing Credits

Dona Herweck Rice, *Editor-in-Chief*; Lee Aucoin, *Creative Director*; Don Tran, *Print Production Manager;* Timothy J. Bradley, *Illustration Manager*; Chris McIntyre, *Editorial Director*; James Anderson, *Associate Editor*; Jamey Acosta, *Associate Editor*; Jane Gould, *Editor*; Peter Balaskas, *Editorial Administrator*; Neri Garcia, *Senior Designer*; Stephanie Reid, *Photo Editor*; Rachelle Cracchiolo, M.S.Ed., *Publisher*

Image Credits

cover Eliza Snow/iStockphoto; p.1 Eliza Snow/iStockphoto; p.4 (left foreground) Lee Torrens/Shutterstock, (left background) NASA, (right) Kochneva Tetyana/Shutterstock; p.5 Lynn Watson/Shutterstock; p.6 juliengrondin/Shutterstock; p.7 Todd Mestemacher/Shutterstock; p.8 Alex Jackson/Shutterstock; p.9 (top) Mana Photo/Shutterstock, (bottom) Li Chaoshu/Shutterstock; p.10 Vidux/Shutterstock; p.11 Oleg F/Shutterstock; p.12 Oleg F/Shutterstock; p.13 PhotoAlto/SuperStock; p.14 MADDRAT/Shutterstock; p.15 Josef Mohyla/Shutterstock; p.16 Beth Van Trees/Shutterstock; p.17 (background) Alexey Skachkov/Shutterstock; p.18 (background) Infomages/Dreamstime.com, (foreground) Elzbieta Sekowska/Shutterstock; p.19 Ken Karp/Digital Light Source/Newscom; p.20 (left) eva serrabassa/iStockphoto, (right) paul benefield/Shutterstock; p.21 (foreground) Darren Hedges/Shutterstock; p.22 Grafissimo/iStockphoto; p.23 Joe Kucharski/Shutterstock; p.24 (left) Leene/Shutterstock, (middle) Jay Crihfield / Shutterstock, (right) cloki/Shutterstock; p.25 (middle) Alan J. Goulet/iStockphoto, (right) Eliza Snow/iStockphoto; p.26 Jaywarren79/Shutterstock; p.27 (background) Hemera Technologies/Ablestock, (top foreground) Charles Shapiro/Shutterstock, (bottom foreground) Smit/Shutterstock; p.28 Rocket400 Studio/Shutterstock; p.29 Ana Clark; p.32 (left) Roberto Danovaro, (right) Roberto Danovaro

Teacher Created Materials
5301 Oceanus Drive
Huntington Beach, CA 92649-1030
http://www.tcmpub.com

ISBN 978-1-4333-1416-2

Table of Contents

All About Matter. 4

States of Matter 6

All About Gas 16

What a Gas! 26

Appendices 28

Lab: What Is Evaporation? . . . 28

Glossary 30

Index 31

A Scientist Today. 32

All About Matter

What is **matter**? Matter is what everything is made of.

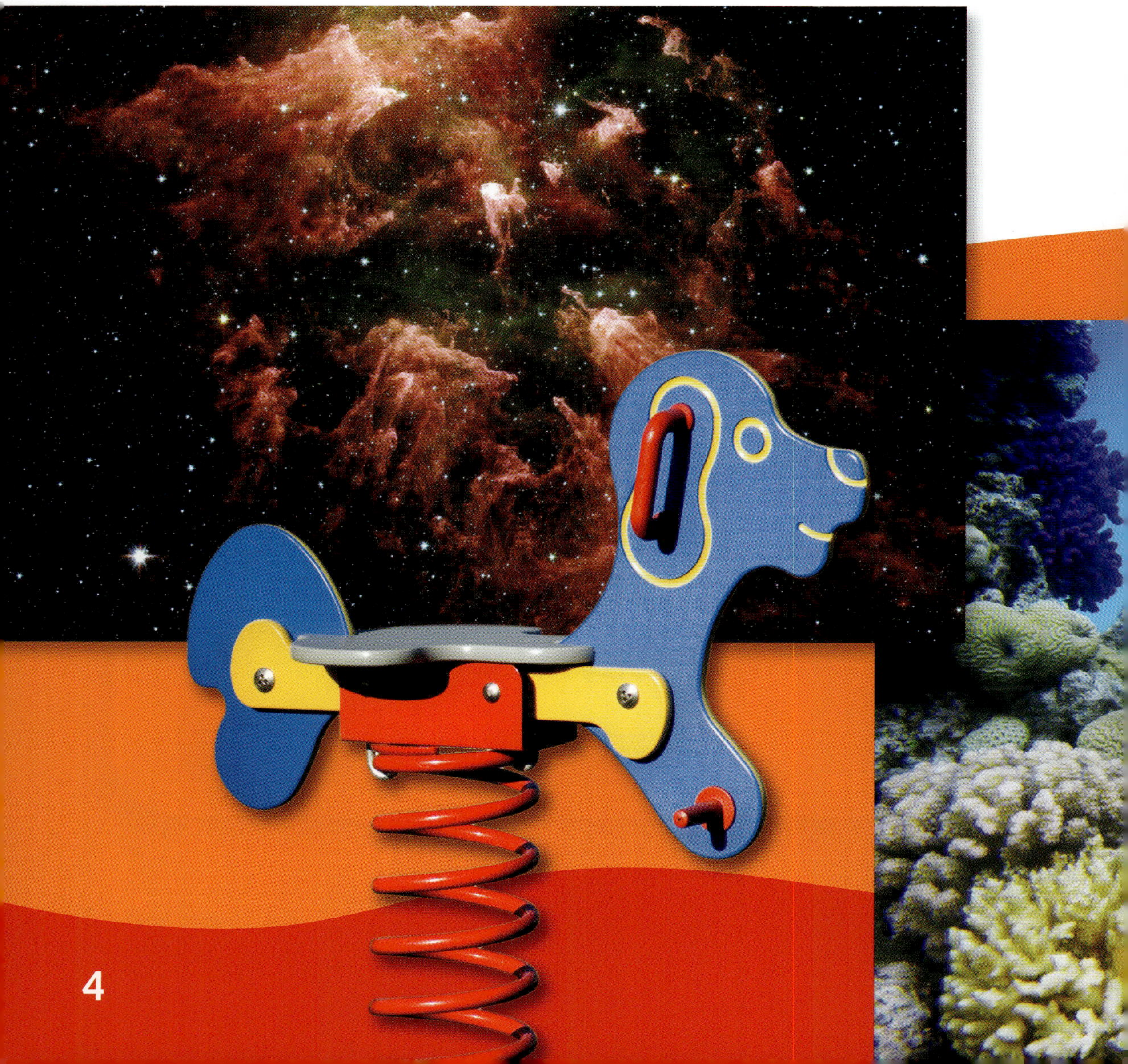

Things that we see, hear, smell, taste, and touch are made of matter. This page is made of matter. You are made of matter. Look up. What do you see? Whatever it is, it is made of matter, too!

Everything is made of matter.

States of Matter

There are three **states of matter**. The first is solid. A solid is like ice or rock. The second is liquid. A liquid is like water or lava. The third is gas. A gas is like air or steam.

You can see gas, liquid, and solid in this scene. Can you pick them out?

All matter is made of **particles** (PAR-ti-kuhls). Particles are very tiny parts. The parts can be close together or far apart. They can move around a lot or be quite still. How close they are and how they move helps to decide the state of matter they form.

There is the most space between the particles of a gas.

liquid

solid

Matter can change. Heat changes matter. Heat makes a solid melt. The solid becomes a liquid. Heat makes a liquid **evaporate** (i-VAP-uh-reyt). The liquid becomes a gas.

This steam is evaporating from the heated water.

Iron can be heated, melted, and molded into tools.

Particles start to move apart when matter is heated. Heat changes the matter's state.

Cold can change matter, too. Cold can make a liquid freeze. The liquid becomes a solid. Cold can turn a gas to a liquid. That is called **condensation** (kon-den-SEY-shun).

Cold turned the water to ice, so this polar bear can have a ride!

You see condensation every time you take a hot bath. The steam in the air hits the cool mirror. The gas becomes a liquid.

A state of matter also depends on its **properties**. Properties are how something looks, feels, or acts.

How do you know that this is a gas?

The properties of a gas are what make it a gas. Does it take up space? Does it have weight? Does it keep its shape? These answers will tell you about some of the properties of gas.

All About Gas

One property is shape. The particles of a gas are spread apart. That means that a gas does not have a set shape. The shape changes by how much space it has.

Gas spreads out to fill up its space.

When matter is solid the particles are close together. When matter is liquid the particles are farther apart. When matter is gas the particles are farthest apart.

Another property is **volume**. Volume is the amount of space that something takes up. A gas spreads out as big as it can. Its volume changes by the size of its container.

A container holds something. This jar is a container. It holds a solid. Unlike gas, a solid stays in its container.

Gas escapes its container if it can.

If you heat up water, it becomes a gas. The gas takes up more volume than the water. Water has more volume when it changes to steam.

Fun Fact

You breathe a gas every day. The gas is air!

Pressure from steam makes this train go. The volume of gas (steam) helps to make the pressure.

Another property is weight. Does a gas have weight? Take a balloon and blow air into it. Does the balloon weigh more than it did before? Yes, but barely. Gases have very little weight. It seems like they do not weigh anything at all.

If balloons were filled with liquids or solids, they would not be light enough to float.

See if you can answer all these questions about gases. Do gases have shape? Do they have weight? Do they take up space?

Can you see the signs of gas in each of these pictures?

Gases take the shapes of their containers. They weigh very little. And they take up all the space they can!

What a Gas!

We need gases to live. Every time you breathe, you breathe in gas. You breathe out gas, too. You may not always see it, smell it, or hear it, but gas is there. Gases are everywhere!

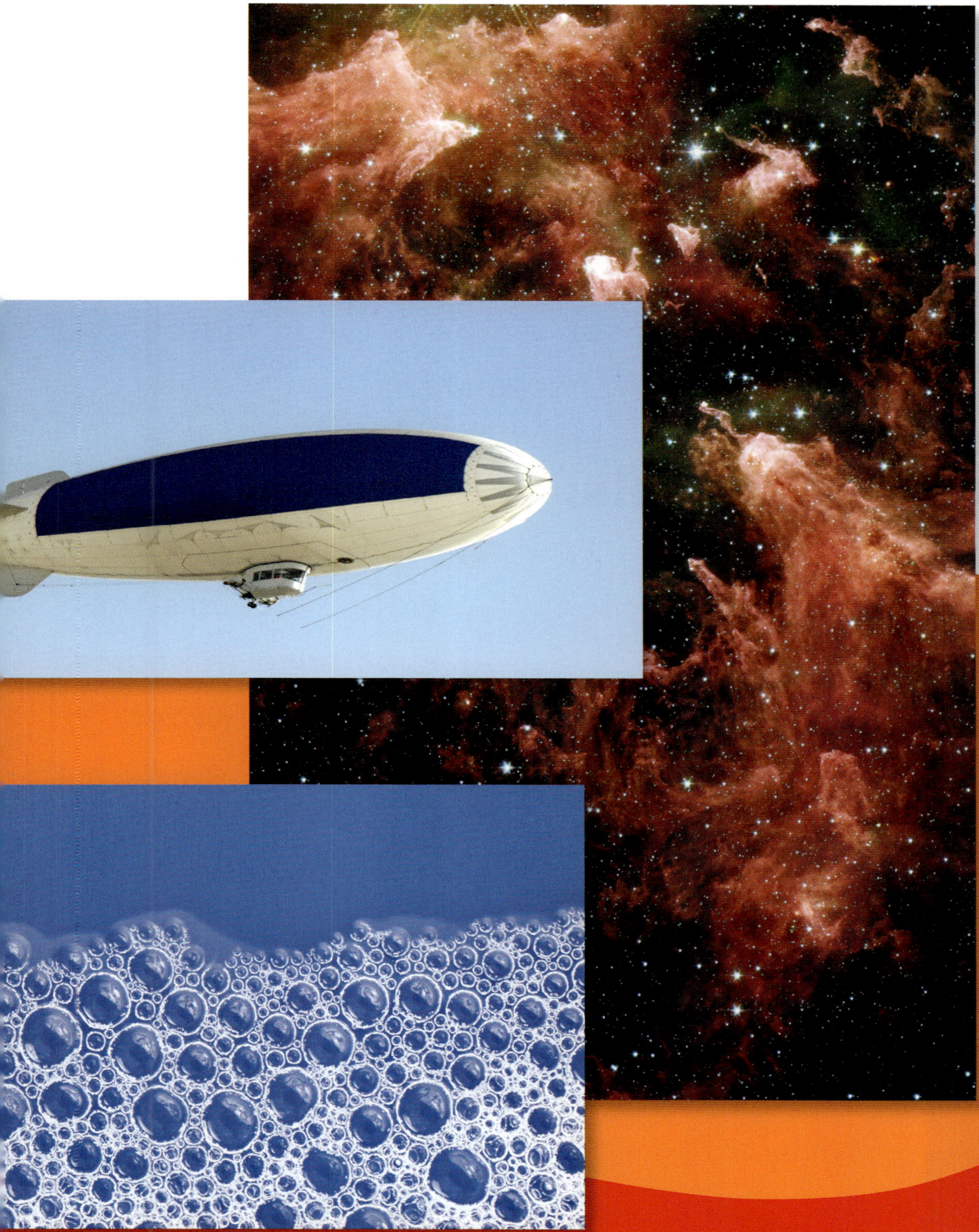

Science Lab: What Is Evaporation?

You can see evaporation in action if you follow these steps.

Materials:

- 2 clear plastic cups
- marker
- plastic wrap
- water
- a sunny day

Procedure:

1. Fill each cup with water. Be sure the cups have the same amount of water.
2. Put plastic wrap tightly over one cup.
3. Mark the water line on both cups.
4. Place the cups outside in the sun where nothing will knock them over.

5 Check the cups after two hours. Did the water go down in either cup? Mark the new water line.

6 Check again in two more hours. Mark the water line again.

7 Keep checking over time. You will see that the cup that is not covered is losing its water. But the water did not spill. It evaporated in the heat of the sun. The plastic covering does not allow the water from the second cup to evaporate, so it should all still be there.

Glossary

condensation—the act of changing a gas to a liquid

evaporate—to change from a liquid to a gas

matter—anything that takes up space

particles—the tiny parts of something

properties—the ways that an object looks, feels, and acts

states of matter—the different forms that matter can take, including solid, liquid, and gas

volume—amount of space something takes up

Index

cold, 12

condensation, 12–13

evaporate, 10

heat, 10–11, 20

matter, 4–5, 8, 10–12, 17

particles, 8, 16–17

properties, 14–23

shape, 15–16, 24

states of matter, 6, 8, 14

volume, 18, 20–21

A Scientist Today

Roberto Danovaro lives in Italy. He is a scientist who studies sea animals. He found the first multi-cell animal we know that lives without oxygen! It lives in the mud on the ocean floor.

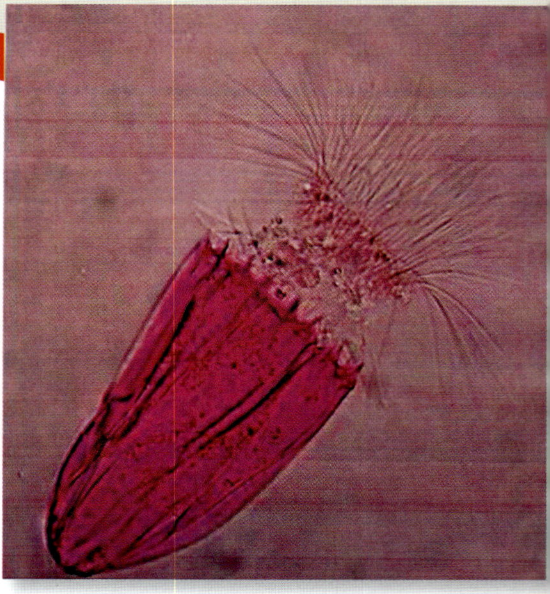